HOW DO WE USE LIGHT?

by Emily Raij

PEBBLE
a capstone imprint

Published by Pebble, an imprint of Capstone.
1710 Roe Crest Drive, North Mankato, Minnesota 56003
capstonepub.com

Library of Congress Cataloging-in-Publication Data is available on the Library of Congress website.
ISBN 9781663970640 (hardcover)
ISBN 9781666325072 (paperback)
ISBN 9781666325089 (ebook pdf)

Summary: What is light? Where does it come from? How does it help us see? Readers investigate and read straightforward text accompanied by vibrant photos to learn all about light.

Image Credits
Capstone Studio: Karon Dubke, 1, 6, (top), 7, 8, 11, HL Studios, 19; Getty Images: JGI/Jamie Grill, 21, Thomas De Wever, 27; Shutterstock: AK-GK Studio, cover, Amorn Suriyan, 29, anatoliy_gleb, 4, Aphelleon, 22, Damsea, 15, Daniel Jedzura, 14, Elena Elisseeva, 5, 26, Freer, 6 (bottom right), Kochneva Tetyana, 25, Lopolo, 17, NDanko, 6 (bottom left), Shotmedia, 28, sirikorn thamniyom, 18, Tish1, 13

Editorial Credits
Editor: Erika L. Shores; Designer: Dina Her; Media Researcher: Jo Miller; Production Specialist: Tori Abraham

TABLE OF CONTENTS

Words in **bold** are in the glossary.

A LIGHT INVESTIGATION

Imagine you are camping. The sun has gone down. Only the moon and stars light up the sky. The campfire crackles. Marshmallows roast over the fire. Then everyone grabs flashlights to tell ghost stories.

In the morning, the sun comes up. It sparkles on the lake. Your shadow follows you as you hike. Time to rest under a shady tree.

Sun, moon, stars, fire, and shadows. What do all of these things have in common besides camping? It's light!

Let's do a light investigation. Choose three objects. One should be clear like a glass. Another should be harder to see through like a piece of wax paper. The last object should be impossible to see through, such as a plastic toy.

drinking glass

wax paper

toy dinosaur

Go in a dark room. Hold a flashlight so it shines a few feet away on an empty wall.

Put each object in front of the flashlight. Does light shine through? Are there shadows on the wall?

What happens to the shadows as you move each object closer to the flashlight? What happens when you move things farther away?

You just did a light experiment! Different types of objects let different amounts of light through. Shadows change as objects move closer to or farther away from a light source.

The glass is **transparent**, or clear. It lets light through completely. Wax paper is **translucent**. Some light shines through. The toy dinosaur is **opaque**. It lets no light through.

When light is blocked by an opaque object, shadows form behind that object. A shadow is the area where light is blocked.

Shadows grow bigger when the object moves closer to the light. They also get fuzzier. Shadows become smaller and sharper as the object moves away from the light.

WHAT IS LIGHT?

Light is energy we can see. Energy makes things move, grow, or change. Heat and sound are other types of energy.

We need light to see. Plants need light to grow. People need plants for food. They give us energy.

Light always comes from a source. It can be a natural source like the sun or fire. The sun is the brightest and most important light source we have.

Many light sources are made by people. Light bulbs are the most common. We also use matches and candles. When the sun goes down at night, we need other light sources to see.

Some animals make their own light. That is called **bioluminescence**. Chemicals inside animals' bodies make them glow. Moon jellyfish and fireflies make their own light. Animals use this light to communicate. They attract mates with it. They use it to find food and escape attackers too.

HOW DO WE SEE LIGHT?

Most things don't make their own light. How can we see them? Light from the sun or other sources shines onto objects. These light waves move in straight paths called rays.

Rays travel until they hit something. Some light is **absorbed**. The rest is **reflected**. Reflected light bounces off the object. Light waves reach our eyes.

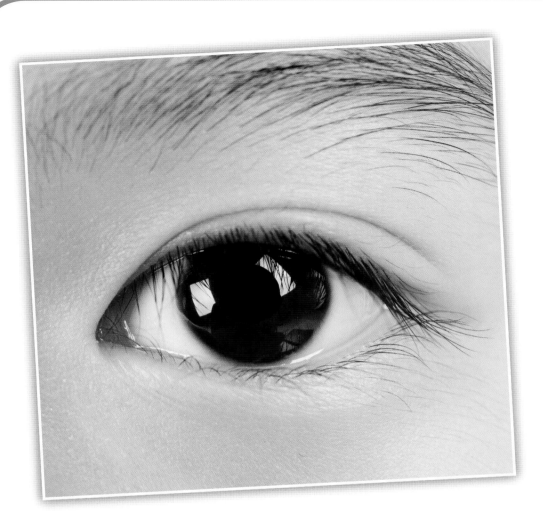

Light enters the eye through the **pupil**. The pupil changes size to control how much light enters. It grows to let in more light. It shrinks to let in less.

Next, light passes through the **lens**. The lens changes shape to focus light. That makes light clearer. A lens gets thicker to make close objects easier to see. It gets thinner to make far objects more visible.

The focused light shows an image on our **retina**. It sends signals through the **optic nerve** to our brain. Our brain then tells us what we're seeing.

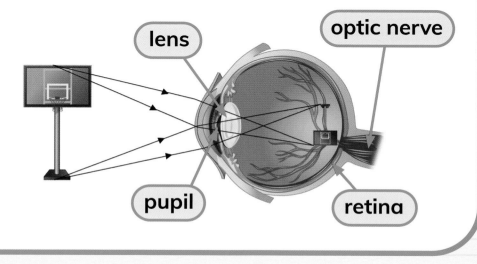

lens

optic nerve

pupil

retina

Think about looking into a still pond. What about looking into a blank phone screen? You will see your reflection looking back at you. When light shines onto smooth, shiny surfaces, we see a perfect reflection. That's how mirrors show us exactly what we look like.

When light shines on rough surfaces, rays bounce off in different directions. We do not see a reflection.

The sun, moon, and stars are far away. How can we see their light? Light is very fast. It travels 186,000 miles (300,000 kilometers) per second to reach Earth. On Earth, light moves more slowly. Air and water slow it down.

The sun is 93 million miles (150 million km) away from Earth. It takes 8 minutes and 20 seconds for sunlight to reach Earth. The moon glows too but doesn't make its own light. It reflects light from the sun.

HOW DO WE SEE COLORS?

Light waves have different wavelengths. That is the distance from the top of one light wave to the top of the next.

Wavelengths make the colors we see. Longer wavelengths make red and orange. Shorter ones make blue and purple. All wavelengths mixed together make white light like the sun.

A **spectrum** is the range of short to long wavelengths. Violet has the shortest. Red has the longest. Orange, yellow, green, and blue are in the middle.

Objects get their color from absorbing or reflecting certain wavelengths. Most objects absorb more than one color. A blue ball reflects blue light. All other colors get absorbed.

Objects that reflect all light look white. They also reflect heat energy. Objects that absorb all light and reflect no light look black. They absorb heat too. That is why a black parking lot feels hotter than a white sidewalk.

HOW DO WE USE LIGHT?

We turn lights on or off. We make them dimmer or brighter. Traffic lights tell drivers to stop or go.

Mirrors change the paths of light rays. This lets us see around opaque objects like walls. Curving mirrors makes objects appear larger and closer or smaller and farther away.

　　We can bend light with lenses. This lets us see better. Eyeglasses, microscopes, and telescopes are all curved, transparent lenses. Light helps us communicate and see the world around us.

GLOSSARY

absorb (ab-ZORB)—to take something in

bioluminescence (buy-oh-loo-muh-NES-uhnss)—the production of light by a living thing

lens (LENZ)—the clear part of the eye behind the pupil and iris that focuses rays of light on the retina to form clear images

opaque (oh-PAKE)—not see-through; blocking all rays of light

optic nerve (OP-tik NURV)—a thin fiber that sends messages from the eye to the brain

pupil (PYOO-puhl)—the round, dark center of your eye that lets in light

reflect (ri-FLEKT)—to return light from an object

retina (RET-uhn-uh)—the lining inside the back of the eyeball

spectrum (SPEK-trum)—a rainbow effect that results from the breakdown of white light

translucent (trans-LOO-suhnt)—letting light pass through but not transparent; frosted and stained glass are translucent

transparent (transs-PAIR-uhnt)—clear; letting light through

READ MORE

Higgins, Melissa. *Light*. North Mankato, MN: Capstone, 2020.

Lundgren, Julie K. *Light: Energy We Can See!* New York: Crabtree Publishing, 2022.

Thiel, Kristin. *Investigating Light and Sound Through Modeling*. New York: Cavendish Square Publishing, 2020.

INTERNET SITES

Learn About Light
sciencewithme.com/learn-about-light/

Light for Kids
sciencekids.co.nz/light.html

Science of Light
ducksters.com/science/light.php

INDEX

ABOUT THE AUTHOR

Emily Raij has written more than 40 books for children and edited dozens of professional resources for K-12 teachers. She lives in Florida with her husband, daughter, son, and dog.